T0197571

An Easter Remembrance

Marcia J. Williams

Illustrated by Damian J. Williams

To order additional copies of this book, contact:
Xlibris
1-888-795-4274
www.Xlibris.com
Orders@Xlibris.com

ISBN: Softcover   978-1-7960-9937-9
         EBook   978-1-7960-9936-2

Print information available on the last page

Rev. date: 06/05/2020

Scripture quotations are from the King James Version of the Holy Bible

Authorized Version

In memory of Deacon Robert L. Williams, my husband, best friend, and greatest supporter, and my mother, Mrs. Elizabeth R. Jenkins, my biggest encourager....

To my children and grandchildren, you have accomplished so much. I am godly proud of you.

Introduction

An Easter Remembrance, is a 20 minute skit for children and youth 4-12 years of age.

In four short scenes, the author highlights the events from the betrayal, crucifixion, death, resurrection, and ascension of Jesus Christ. The majority of the skit is told by the narrator.

The skit reminds us that these events in and surrounding the resurrection are the very foundation of the Christian's belief.

This skit is intended to be used as an evangelistic outreach tool.

-Marcia J. Williams

Cast of Characters:

Narrators- Two young adults

Jesus

Disciple- Scene I

Judas- Scene 1

Crowd- a mixture of children at the cross scene

Child #1

Child #2

Child #3

Child #4

Thief #1

Thief#2

Disciple #1 (on road to Emmaus)

Disciple #2 (on road to Emmaus)

Angel #1

Angel #2

Props/Costumes:

- Chair

- Robes, sheets, or biblical costumes for each child. Large pieces of material placed over the shoulders and belted or tied at the waist are suggested.

- 3 free standing wooden crosses 4 or 5 ft. tall on a base

- 2 pairs of angel wings

Scene I:

THE PASSOVER MEAL AND LAST SUPPER

Based upon Mathew 26

Narrator: During the week Jesus was to be crucified, he entered Jerusalem. It was the time of the Jewish Passover Feast. The religious leaders had gathered in the palace of Caiaphas, the High Priest, to plan how they might take Jesus and kill him. Judas agreed to deliver Jesus into their hands for 30 pieces of silver.

Narrator: Meanwhile, Jesus and the disciples made ready to eat the Passover Meal and take the Lord's Supper. It was on the night Jesus was betrayed. While they were eating, Jesus said,

Jesus: (seated before the audience-points toward the audience) Verily, I say unto you, that one of you shall betray me.

Narrator: The disciples became sorrowful, and many began to speak.

Disciple: Lord, is it I?

Judas: Master, is it I?

Jesus: (speaks again sadly) He that dips his hand with me in the dish shall betray me.

Judas' Betrayal of Jesus

The Passover Meal and Last Supper

Scene II:

THE CRUCIFIXION

(Jesus and the two thieves stand in front of the three crosses with their arms stretched out. The crowd passes by Jesus mocking Him)

Narrator: Jesus was betrayed by Judas, one of his disciples and eventually, placed into the hands of the religious leaders.

Narrator: Jesus had done nothing wrong. He had committed no sin, but received no justice. After a mockery of a trial, he was taken to a place outside Jerusalem called Golgotha or Calvary. There he was crucified along with two thieves.

Narrator: People passed by taunting, and mocking Him.

Child#1: Save thyself.

Child#2: If you are the Son of God, come down from the cross

Child #3: He saved others. Himself he cannot save!

Child #4: I thought you were the King of the Jews. Come down, Jesus, and we will believe you.

Thief #2 (looking towards Jesus): Lord, remember me when thou comest into thy kingdom.

Jesus: Today, shalt thou be with me in paradise.

The Crucifixion Site

Scene III:

THE ROAD TO EMMAUS

(Two disciples and Christ walking on the road to Emmaus)

Based upon Luke 24

Narrator: After Jesus' death and resurrection, He made many appearances to his disciples to show them that he had indeed risen from the dead. Two who he appeared to were walking to a city called Emmaus.

(Jesus comes up beside the disciples as they are walking and begins to walk with them)

Narrator: At first when Jesus came up to them, they did not recognize him. Sh-sh-sh-sh, let's listen to their conversation…

Disciple # 1: Many things have happened in Jerusalem these past three days.

Jesus (begins walking beside them): What is it you're talking about? and why are you so sad?

Disciple #2: Are you a stranger in Jerusalem? Haven't you heard of all the things that happened this week concerning Jesus of Nazareth?

Disciple #1: Yes, we had thought he was the Messiah come from God to rescue Israel. However, the religious leaders arrested him and had him crucified.

Narrator: When they got to the village of Emmaus, the disciples invited Jesus to stay with them. It was when Jesus ate with them that their eyes were opened. (Disciples stand towards Jesus looking at him in amazement) They recognized him- it was Jesus- HE was alive! He had RISEN!

Two Disciples and Christ walking on the road to Emmaus

Scene IV:

JESUS' ASCENSION BACK TO HEAVEN

(2 angels enter and stand before the audience as the narrator speaks)

Based upon Acts 1

Narrator: 40 days after his resurrection Jesus was gathered with his disciples. After he had spoken many things with them concerning the kingdom of God, he was taken up from them into heaven. As the disciples stood watching, Jesus was taken up and a cloud received him out of their sight. Two angels stood by them in white garments.

Angel#1 (turns to audience): Why stand ye gazing up into heaven?

This same Jesus which is taken up from you into heaven shall come again in the same manner one day.

THE END

Jesus Ascension Back To Heaven

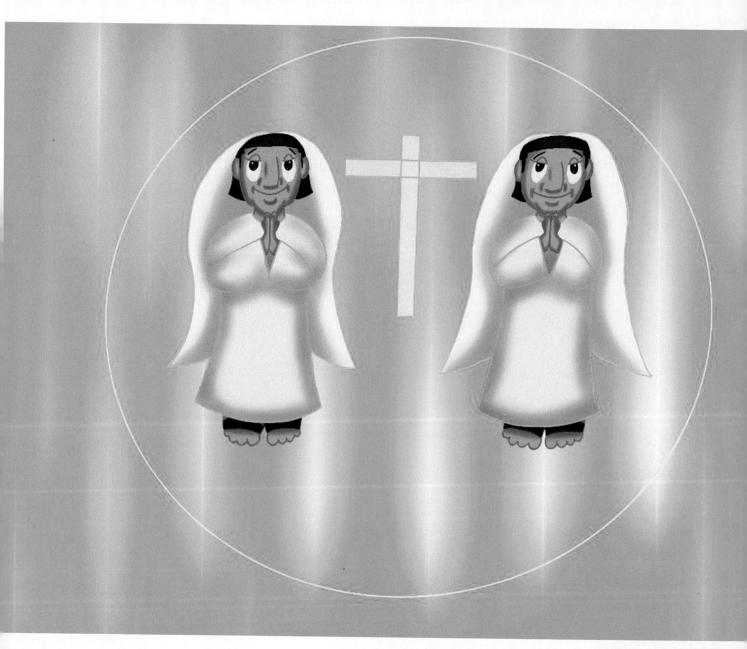

The Two Angels

Narrator: Jesus Christ came and died for our sins and arose so that we may have life. Say this simple prayer to receive Him as your Lord and Saviour:

"Jesus come into my heart. Forgive me of all my sins. Come into my heart and be my Lord and Saviour".

Amen

About the Author

<u>*Marcia J. Williams*</u>, has been a published author since 2013. This is her second literary work. She was a children's instructor at her local church. Marcia is a retired healthcare laboratory professional, and a mother and grandmother. More than anything, she is a prayer warrior.

Printed in the United States
By Bookmasters